Mother Tongue

Mother Tongue

Selected poems by Pura López Colomé

Translated by Lorna Shaughnessy

ARLEN
HOUSE

First published on 27 April 2006 by Arlen House

PO Box 222
Galway
Ireland
Phone/fax: 353 86 8207617
Email: arlenhouse@gmail.com

ISBN 1–903631–32–7, *paperback*

L164.745 1861
€12.00 COL

Ireland Literature Exchange
Idirmhalartán Litríocht Éireann

the arts
council
schomhairle
ealaíon

Cover image courtesy of Barrie Cooke
Typesetting by Arlen House
Printed by ColourBooks, Dublin

CONTENTS

10   Acknowledgements

11   Preface   *Mary O'Malley*

13   Translator's Note

Part I: Among Volcanoes

19   *Dramatis Personae*
20   *Stricto Sensu*
21   Heartache
22   Precision Balance
23   Soothsayer
25   Prism
28   Dreaming of Star Music
30   Article of Faith
31   Among Volcanoes

Part II: Cradle-Song

35   Brief Episode
36   Cradle-Song
43   Painstaking
47   Cotton
49   Foundling
53   Passing Through

Part III: Sacrifice

57   King
60   Sacrifice
61   Epimone
62   Sweetness
65   Schism
66   *Et in secula seculorum*
67   The Snow-White Falls of Niagara

Part I: Entre volcanes

73   *Dramatis Personae*
74   *Stricto Sensu*
75   Dolor de corazón
76   El fiel de la balanza
77   Arúspice
79   Prisma
82   Sueño de música estelar
84   Artículo de fe
85   Entre volcanes

Part II: Canción de cuna

89   Breve episodio
90   Canción de cuna
97   A duras penas
101   Algodón
103   Adoptivo
107   De paso

Part III: Sacrificio

111   Rey
114   Sacrificio
115   Epímone
116   Dulzura
119   Cisma
120   *Et in secula seculorum*
121   Níveas cataratas de Niágara

127   Poems and their sources

... she would only emerge
through her mother and tongue,
the one true oracle ...'
                    Sweetness

Acknowledgements

The Publisher gratefully acknowledges the financial assistance of Ireland Literature Exchange (Translation Fund), Dublin, Ireland
www.irelandliterature.com
info@irelandliterature.com

Arlen House wishes to thank Pura López Colomé for permission to reproduce her poems, Mary O'Malley for her Preface and Barrie Cooke for the original artwork for the book cover.

The translator wishes to thank Pura López Colomé and Olwen Rowe for their generous support of the translation process.

Mary O'Malley

Preface

Pura López Colomé was born among volcanoes and fire blazes through her work, iced always by her intellect. Her poetry is marked by an intellectual rigour and a relentless interrogation of language which demand exacting methods of translation. I did some translations with her some years back and her poems do not shed their layers of mystery easily, though the process of translating her was always fascinating since she is her own strictest taskmaster. Rendering Spanish poems into English without losing the poetry requires a particular relationship with metaphor, with the canon and above all a willingness to forsake the narrative and enter the world of dream with its less obvious associations. Perhaps it is helpful to refer here to Gaston Bachelard's discussion of the place in poetry of "… direct images of matter. Vision names them, but the hand knows them".

Pura López's poetry sustains an intense interrogation of language, of experience and of the ocean below the surface of the world she inhabits. It speaks of a rich interior life, delivered to us with clear everyday metaphors. In "Soothsayer":

> There was once a rope
> someone threw us,
> and food we devoured
> without so much as tasting it.

Rope and food enable the poem to negotiate safely the abstractions of "this fog, this fate" and "desire".

"Stricto sensu" and "Precision Balance" are my personal favourites in this selection, and since one of the purposes of translation is to send the reader back to the original text, I may have different pets by the time this book is in print. I read each poem in both Spanish and English, interested in how the poetic associations are made, now deep under the surface of the language, now held up, faceted, to the light.

In "Painstaking" the delightful question: "Who is raining?" sets the tone for an intimate, powerful sequence on grief, with its image of woman as fertile, aquatic being, shedding herself painfully in tears. Translating these poems into English without losing either the clarity or the intention of the originals is a difficult and engaging task, but not thankless.

Lorna Shaughnessy has done Trojan work in presenting us with this sequence of López Colomé's poems, and I am delighted that Arlen House is making this important Mexican poet available in Ireland.

Translator's Note

Risk-taking is a fundamental part of the process of translation. In the case of these translations of Pura López Colomé's poems, the element of risk was perhaps greater for Pura than for myself. She is an established poet in Mexico and an experienced translator whose work is known and highly regarded in Latin America, North America and Europe. Her decision to trust these poems to an inexperienced translator has presented me with both a challenge and an opportunity. I am grateful for the impeccable propriety of her responses to my queries throughout the process; her ability to provide just enough information to clarify questions of context or tone, while insisting that the translated poem reflect the decisions and choices made by the translator. Inevitably, I have learned many things about myself as a translator along the way.

There are poems in this selection such as "Foundling" or "Painstaking" that I would not have attempted to translate were it not for Pura's prodding, her willingness to live with the outcomes, whatever they were, of my gambles. The greatest challenge to the translator posed by these and other poems in the selection, is the pervasiveness of wordplay, reflecting the self-conscious nature of this poet's relationship with her medium. Her constant probing of language and exploration of etymology underline the intellectual and ontological quest for meaning in all her work. I am aware that Pura feels she has always "belonged" more to language than to geographical place. The foregrounding of this debt to *mother tongue* in her poems was what inspired the title of the book: that sense of mother tongue as source, origin, identity, consolation and repository of meaning.

I have not always been able to find suitable 'equivalents' for Pura's wordplay in my translations, and the immediacy of the etymological links between Latin and Spanish is often lost. But where I have been unable to capture the wordplay in a particular line or juxtaposition, I have sought to compensate by inserting an element of wordplay elsewhere in the same poem. In "Foundling", for example, I have translated the euphemistic sense of *adoptivo* with the English *foundling*. However the semantic and grammatical subtlety of the distinction between *adoptivo* and *adoptado* in Spanish is lost. In the same poem, Pura's playful use of the diminutive suffix in Spanish is not easily rendered in English. I have exploited the diminutive *ling* suffix of *foundling* early in the poem, and later, where the diminutive forms referring to a chick and its mother are used in the Spanish, have resorted to the kind of nouns associated with babies (or rather, the way adults speak to babies) such as *mammy* and *birdie*. My hope is that these words, combined with the alliterative effect of *mammy/morsel/mouthful*, will reproduce a compensatory effect, perhaps reminiscent of a nursery rhyme, in keeping with the poem's subject-matter.

This combination of playfulness and intellectual quest is for me one of the most striking qualities of Pura's work. Also her keen awareness of the sharp contrast between the scale of the physical world we inhabit and human fragility, captured so acutely in the poems "Among Volcanoes" and "King". I am conscious of the importance of the Central Mexican landscape in her work, the way that landscape acts a physical reminder of the epic sweep of geological time that dwarfs human existence and endeavour.

Pura once described her poems to me as "flechas de lento penetrar" (slowly-penetrating arrows). Through them we can observe the archer's deadly accuracy with the 'slow motion' of a mind in the process of reflection. The process of translating them has been one of reading in 'slow motion' and reflecting on the nature of memory, the inescapability of the past and the possibility – or not – of consolation. These are poems that deliberately and uncompromisingly resist comfortable answers. The language in the original poems is pared back to an apparent essence, without losing a single layer of potential meaning. For a translation to yield even a fraction of their resonances represents quite a challenge. I am grateful that my own inexperience hid this fact from me when I embarked on this journey, allowing me to take risks in a state of blissful ignorance and learn as much as I have in the process.

Among Volcanoes

Dramatis personae

My voice slowly found the weave
of its own fabric. Stopped.
Believed it could stretch no farther,
then did just that.
And discovered in this way a source
never before spoken of,
a place it unknowingly
belonged to,
to which it would later return,
opening doors,
priming the inner ear.
A shell from untiring sea-swells
meeting every desire,
entering the body
in a red intensity.

Then your voice, a blizzard
from the highest branches
of wintering woodland,
from orchards in the tundra,
holm oak, cedar
and tamarind,
pulsing through the wakeful
as they walk,
savouring
the melodic aridity
of thunder.

Stricto sensu

*"I remember little of significance from my
private life."*
INGMAR BERGMAN

In the strictest sense, I am born
bathed in the light of a hallowed presence.
Marked out between the index and ring finger
of my right hand,
above the bulge of muscle that protects
the last phalanx.
A mountain made Mohammed find his path.
And no matter how I cling to the Sierra Madre,
another magnetic force drags me, counting down
the minutes and seconds
to where I was not me.
Where I was no more than a pulsing ocean,
ever-calming, persisting,
never touching the flaming core.
The idea of home and hearth,
making a commotion of the happiest moments,
dolls, things scattered about, instruments of deception
beneath the gaze of two powerful images: the Immaculate
    Conception
and Teresa the little flower with her odourless branch.
The awareness of anger.

Making my way to sadness was like entering a room.
And I closed the door. Lock and key. Chains
and padlocks. And I uttered the word inscrutable.
And I found untranslatable the torrent
of indelible ink.

Why do you wander in solitude
amid the fleet and camp
in the immortal night?
(ILIAD, X, 139)

The lake of the dead has no end.
Also known as a river, the great Styx,
it flows softly, softly,
beguiling believers and the wise.
A bed of dreams, of whisperings,
nestling snugly in nooks and crannies:
a mirage of human labyrinths
cut adrift.

I sense beginnings in this boat, I pondered.
Its timbers have left marks on my hands,
the night's oars are slowly spinning
the horizon's true chrysalis.

Is this the vortex, the water's eye
where the goddess sank her son
to render him invulnerable,
savage, indifferent?
Is this the dry-eyed Word
that casts shields overboard?

Precision balance

For Thomas Kinsella, the perfectionist

Ghostly hands wrapped
this stone island
in a rainforest luxuriance, covering
each convex surface with its sheen.

Someone had lost their memory:
the great summoner of melancholy,
sole impulse behind each act of initiation,
writer of the epic.
His obliging spirit put right the wound,
giving in exchange his own voice.

That evening, he showed me a scar
and said: fill me with fire.
Let the dawn shatter
the iris,
and with each breath
conjure up
its colour.

Soothsayer

I dreamt again that I was in a tube
with smooth walls, obra magna,
plunging into its depths,
into my own presence:
God be with you,
words heard from afar.
Now I am falling into clearsightedness,
into an awareness
that we never did surface
as I once believed we did;
and the faces back then
– oh my childhood –
that we saw as distorted reflections
on the warped metal of a wall,
were a distillation of the future.

There was once a rope
someone threw us,
and food we devoured
without so much as tasting it.

There was once a last crust of bread
caressing the maddened palate,
but mostly there were words, rebounding,
the only things to touch the farthest shore of light.
Reaching out then withdrawing,
this faithful gift, this unblemished
to-ing and fro-ing, ours alone.

I dreamt of eternity as well.
Where all creatures could roam
on and off their beaten tracks,
with no tubular walls,
promising litanies
sounding between the durings and the whiles.

Very close to the surface
of this fog, this fate,
I felt desire.
I wanted to be saved
inside those untouchable beings.

Nomen est omen,
They were already humming.
Omen est nomen.

Desiring to be among the blessed,
I saw them make their way along the usual path,
the one that leaves the city to go someplace,
some small part of the world,
part of my wounded humanity,
a welcome sight for whoever watches over me,
whoever it is who is within without being me,
in my thirst, my oscillating moments
of tribulation and peace.
I was one of them.
One and of myself.

The pilgrims make their way uphill to Chalma. They
know that the dry branches they carry will flower along
the way. Mostly they are young. They also bring with
them water, a sleeping mat, and the visible trappings of
their everyday lives. There are old people too. Children
carried on shoulders. The shrine advances, in search of its
own location.

Its long history suddenly
awakens in a question.
What do they ask
of this Lord they revere,
or rather,
whose mortified body is glorified
by today's exhaustion,
yesterday's poverty?
Permission to go on crying with rage or impotence,

permission to get sick and worn out,
permission to witness terrifying insufficiency
at the very heart of the horn of abundance,
permission to forget, even,
the seven or eight year-old ghost
that flies, wild,
with neither rhyme nor reason,
and bring it back to earth,
forget future history,
the pointless sacrifices of love?
Is that it?
Oh body, master and Lord,
show me a tree carved in your image,
synagogues, basilicas, mosques
all wrapped in your being.

They have set up camp. Night falls. Groups form, just men here, men and women there, women with babies and small children a little way off. Around the campfire some stand, others squat. They do not share food or coffee – each one brings their own portion – but rather a common purpose … which they celebrate here while they sit on the humble earth, small stones embedding themselves in their thighs, holding a baby to an unconcealed breast. Heat emanates from the nearness of arms, backs, necks, breasts; not from the fire: from their own blood. Some fall asleep, heads nodding, others keep vigil. No need for a roof.

We are all tied
to the rhythm of the stars' breathing
as they sing.
This was the communion of a constellation,

I prayed with terror or envy,
this one rotation
this one passage,
the joy of what is indispensable.
No more, no less.

The following day, still feeling rapture and awe, I
retraced my steps, wanting to inhale again the lingering
fragrances of all that had been dreamed and shared in
that place. Like the pilgrim who returns to touch the
votive stone, the feet or hands of the worn image of a
favourite, miraculous saint.

I found only litter.
The great gaping mouth of the Lord,
the stench of his breath.

Dreaming of Star Music

For Beto and his creatures

I made my way to the window,
drawn by an irresistible force,
but couldn't see enough from there.
I had to go out and meet the skies
of scattered opal
painted with broad brush strokes,
no trace of horizons,
no glimmer of electric lights,
no silhouetted houses, farms,
no human habitation.

Just the murmuring stars
and their visible movement.
I could hear them speak,
and what they said
resonated with snatches
of songs you have sung
and will go on singing
to the end of time.

A personal timbre
that concurs exactly
with the movement,
position and intergalactic transformation
of stars that were born
just so the sustained note of a shadow

that we look to for guidance,
and the short note that answers with the truth,
followed by a necessary silence,
can coincide
with a flicker of light,
no particular reason why,
and even suggest a shape
to the distant eyes of the curious
who look for forms, only forms,
the silhouette
of a bear, a dog or a scorpion,
some recognisable life-form,
unable, poor creatures,
to abandon themselves to the music of the spheres,
the endless
winding
of the simple skein
of spaces such as this.

Article of faith

In the power of the wind to command the dawn
and the miniscule destiny
of a given day.
In the pages and pages that attempt
some class of definition.
While *busyness* growls in the background,
bending ancient trees until they
kiss the sacred earth they stand on.
That sets them alight and feeds them,
contrives their waxing and waning,
the fragile treetop
the teeming foliage,
impossibly high.
Feminine the one, masculine the other,
their defining features now chopped off.

Everything so close.
We advanced defenceless. And reached the summit
where we turned to face one another.
Like Narcissus, our image
multiplied in pools
of self-love,
sublimely old.
Believable.
Article of faith.

Among volcanoes

Born among volcanoes
that appear extinct.
On ground destined to shake.

A shudder. An earthquake.
Someone to-ing and fro-ing
checking if a wall,
a lamp
could come loose and fall
on the sleeping.
We could lose everything.
God willing or not.
Be reduced to a Pompeii.

A naked circumstance
like this winter skylight
has shown me the way
through the fog.
The snow will turn to meltwater
and the light to a denial of fear and atrocity.
The house swallows light on an ancient tongue,
heavenly light in the tongue of ancients,
a window here.
The promised land.
True skylight in the darkness.

Cradle-Song

Brief Episode

You were just describing
a little girl with unkempt hair,
a pained
inward
look,
dirty knees.
Her dress too small
and a knot stopping her throat.
The body she inhabits turns
into something she didn't ask for,
that ends in a full stop.

Cradle-song

on the Ritter-Anguiano scale

The hush-a-bye lull tells a parable.
Smooth, even tones that answer
to the remoteness of the world,
the farthest crack in the cave wall,
this skull. And resonate.

The echo
in your body
all ears.
Cradle-time.

1

A girl, a little girl,
not the kind you meet in nursery rhymes
but dark, too dark for that.
Between her first and second years,
perhaps less. Her ear cocked
for the humming sound that dips in and out
of that time of wonder.
In her *selfness*, she feels
the cool air of the tropical breeze
as it sweeps through the bedroom,
filling the curtains, making them sway
from left to right,
crinolines in the window-frame,
departing boats that forsake their
likeness for a deeper sea
whose waves never break

in the beyond. Let them sail back
again to meet the dawn.
Let there be words,
let light and darkness have names,
certainty and fire:
my love.
My love this, my love that,
the boat rocks,
its wake fanning out
across a glowing face.

Don't cry,
your salt will melt away
the spray.

> *You*
> *are the music on the wind,*
> *a sanctuary for the sands*
> *you came to cross in your bare feet*
> *rather than be burdened with shame.*
> *Let the shadows lighten your load,*
> *let coral and pearl prove true*
> *in this total sea-change.*
>   *Storm.*

2

And if life should thin out,
blood in the oil,
a canvas woven and unravelled
from almost the first
here to there

you to me
mother
to darkness.
From song to wall.
A breeze strokes your face
and lights up the land.
Rope, wool, thread,
your hair twisting
into a knot, a tangle
of dried-out yarn that flies out
to meet passion-filled stories
with no endings.
Muffled voices string together each life's portion,
it's not the sand they capture
but the desert itself,
and we are journeying towards the rain,
towards enchantment,
between healing, falling ill, healing, hush-a-bye
the miracle of seeing again
between one affliction and the next.
Swim, swim, sail out to love.
Sleeping
sail out to meet yourself. Sea-salt,
tears,
mortal spaces.

And like that breeze-creature, later growing to a wind,
you wanted to sip the honey in the place the bees made it,
not settle for less, but know you were the guest
of honour in that banquet in the walled garden,
and like the madman who knows his own madness
fly on the back of a bat,
not a swan or a dove or even a sparrow.
Never mind a crow.

3

So hold on tight here, in this lap,
infant nestling
from birth to death,
emerging only sometimes,
only furtively,
only out of necessity,
to sample the warmth of destiny.

Then out of the breeze, honey and wild flight
comes delight in your birth-voice.

Rest, nobleness,
locked in a tower,
and blink
at scenes worth
the bother.
Prayers over the body,
they begin
to visit you in your casket,
doing the rounds around your likeness
without touching
like fingers sliding over strings,
the milky way
of a lyre, sarcophagus
of the living interred
who have seen a way
to leave behind this place.

Such fine skin, like lace made of rice-paper,
with neither witness
nor history.

4

On the eve of the great battle
there are signs
in windows, on walls
and cloistered floors
where your version of the sublime
was the tongue of an enormous
bronze bell.
You were warned about the journey:
for company you would have
a cradle-song
that you could pluck from inside.
No-one would dare stand in your way:
just this once,
all hands on deck.
With no deaths about you,
unfinished tributes.

So throw open the chests, captain.
Open the windows and be healed.
Be a world fallen silent
where no-one knocks on your door.

5

The final note,
a regal note for winter,
a coldness settling in on itself.
Companion to the questioner
it asks how, with so much anger,
beauty could send up a plea
with only the force

of a flower.
The key to the tower.

     If I were cured,
     if I were well
     if I could just glimpse through that opening
     feeling even fleetingly complete,
     I would risk my health again.
     It would play with me, humming along.
     There are poppies
     that make you beautiful inside,
     between your fields and gardens,
     pleasures unpossessed by lord or master.

Better to pour out magic potions
from these tear-ducts,
let the diseased entrails
weep for joy,
the scythe.

     Unshackled breeze,
     the sweetest morsel that pulls away
     just as the mouth opens.

     6

From the wooden casket,
rosewood or cedar,
guitar, coffer and urn,
a call to the enemy incubates.
This is the time of waiting

for the spell that will set you free,
fill yourself up with intoxicating smells,
harmonise faultlessly
and feel it.

Healing musician,
let this deed be like a flower's.
There is fruit to be had,
bring it to ripeness, the word is yours:

Suscitare, to make move,
return to movement,
put before your own
an ancient will
with all its memories.
The God
of death
sleeps defenceless
in unformed arms.
The cradle calls.

Painstaking

1

Kneeling on a high-backed armchair,
watching the rain.
Who is raining?
It is raining on my sixth year,
and I've just heard it for the first time
properly.
I have just learned
how to split spheres
and stay absolutely still.
Misting up the window pane, I savour
the particular intensities of downpour, storm,
liquid curtain, tempest,
cloudburst,
heavy drops or light:
a dropper-full of measured affection,
a sweating drops of blood.
Some unexpressing self ripples like a flag,
the raining self, the one who makes it an inconjugable act:
I rain, God rains.
On the other side of this cool curtain
my mother is talking to her sister.
She consoles her, for a change.
Because she is a happy woman, happy enough
not to hear the rain,
to feel its presence like an involuntary memory.
Its pit-pit-pattering.

2

Rainfall, dripping on the cement patio
weaves baskets that instantly dissolve.
A little farther off, it conceals a lack of symmetry
on the pond's surface. Everything merges into oneness.
Like man and woman, one and the same flesh.
Delirium, paradise, appear and disappear
between turquoise blue, pearl white,
and the green wing of a fly drifting past,
embedding themselves in my sight,
reverberating.
Like a gunshot.

Then for the first time
a classroom, a school,
a colouring book.
At night I can
not get to sleep.
Too much water and not a tear shed.
Too much that is cast adrift.
I wrap myself in the welcoming blackness.
But I can see everything. Or so I believe.
When I turn over I come face to face with more water,
your blindness.

3

Your eyes are the source of a river of mud, rising in a
relentless, aching rush.
Like a woman gone mad going round in circles.
The rhythmic breath of those who sleep becomes
    intolerable,
those who wake within their sleep. And see in colour.

You switch on the radio. The station gives the exact time
    every minute.
You wish you could go deaf.
Just die and make it all worthwhile.
But no. These bitter tears will flow, *painstaking,*
slapping our faces;
wilfully you exclude yourself, dressing in dark colours,
eating apart, tyrannising with smells, foul or sweet,
without the remotest intention of celebrating anything.
A living scruple. An anti-everything.
An unceasing, mysterious grieving
like Mary's virginity, before, during and after the birth,
this double-edged sword, this ordinary, common or
    garden piece of junk,
"this cruel fate that comes between us".

4

Description is revelation:
if you catch a glimpse of the truth
and plunge right into it
you can make it disappear,
maybe even make it rain
maybe even be the one who rains.
You have to fasten it round your neck
like a hangman's noose,
or a scapular.

Description

The heart is a muscle,
a speaking organ.
It expresses all that goes on outside,

sounding out with drumbeats
in concentric circles,
our many keys.

Revelation

I take off the veil, make you known,
show you on Veronica's clothe.
I imagine myself back
in the peppertree,
that immense tree, with its rough bark
and fruit like a flower, small, round,
almost all skin.
Two children perched in its branches
ask each other things, peel and count the segments
of their curiosity, squeeze the last drop of juice
from what they do and don't understand,
till only the pulp remains in their hands,
their sticky confidante.
From that point the rope was tied
that held up countless piñatas
or swung like a jungle creeper.
I cried out, seeing what was coming,
and when my eyes reached the heavens I saw
the branches of the peppertree in all their glory.
Our secrets
were ambidextrous,
two-faced, scapulars.
We never spoke again the way we did that day.

Cotton

Waves broke on the choppy
seas of cotton fields
in Georgia, Alabama,
a kind of mallow, as my father
so eruditely put it,
whose fruit is a pod
containing several seeds
wrapped in a white down.
I smiled at these details
that seemed to come from
an old botanical manual
with its *ad hoc* engravings,
so different from the cotton-down,
oil-stained, abandoned
in a corner of the garage.
The waves of prodigious cotton
overspilling the pages of Nat Turner's confessions,
the warp and weft of a dress
worn by the young mother
who led me by the hand.
She boarded the bus first.
And so I commenced an endless
journey of haunting detail,
her high-heeled shoes,
seamed stockings
and cotton dress.
Cotton print, lightweight,
suitable for a woman coming from the provinces,
from warmer parts.
Is it new? I asked.
She smiled, but I went back

like a flash to the second floor landing,
her footsteps and the brightly-coloured measuring tape
draped around her neck. The tracing-paper patterns
unfolded on the work-bench.
Say no more.
But listen, listen, and you'll hear
the notes that came floating, just for me,
at the same moment, from the house on the corner
where we began our journey. I turned, and not even
the cotton's snowstorm or its sudden and evocative
    origins
in such peculiarly accented geographies
could distract me from that music and the words:
"Lend your ears to the raising of our voices".
I didn't speak German, and yet I still hear it,
chiselled into my memory
Hore wie wir, die Stimme erheben,
er he-e-e-e-e-E-e-e-e-e-E,
etceteras of a song that tells no lie,
makes no reference to God
or the prayers I would later learn
from the lips of that same woman,
just the blinding
whiteness
of a crop
of cotton,
the cloth that came from it
and the cacophonous patterns of its flowers
printed on the urban sensuality
of another time.

Foundling

When referring to certain children with sad eyes,
bad habits, odd little ways and a stale smell
nothing like *Maja* soap or the *Palmolive* that later
came from the big city and the kind of rearing
God intended,
the term most commonly used
at the table was "foundling".
I considered the semantics.
Found myself skating on the thin ice of dubious
      grammar.
Weren't they referring to a child
who'd been adopted?
Was the passive voice too much to countenance?
To call a child a foundling will always be a different
      matter
than concluding: it was given away.
It lacks that affective, diminutive *ling,*
leaving only a person who came into the world
because no-one knew how to stop it.
Guardians would be strict on grammar.

And how different the stories of those who lived
out the same circumstance, unknowing to a certain point,
a certain age when the revelation of mysteries occurred.
Love: enigma: keys to the kingdom
ex abundantia cordis. The heart missed a beat
at the news. In the best case scenario
they were foundlings. And all that looking for a likeness
between my eyebrows and yours'
or in our hair, in the blink of an eye

turned out to be no more than
"getting your hopes up".

      Around the table,
      four of us.
      Physically, it doesn't
      form a circle,
      but it might as well.
      So much light.
      Looking out on the garden.
      A prism
      needs no explanation.

A few new shoots of lilacs,
some fading daffodils and tentative tulips.
Three trees of similar height or stature,
giant adolescents competing.
The middle one distinguished by
an invasion of ivy forming nooks and crannies
where migratory birds can shelter.
Suddenly:

      Do you see that fat little bird,
      the light brown one?
      The diminutive form
      cheeps.
      It's a chick
      waiting for its mammy
      who, day after day,
      brings it little mouthfuls.
      The size of the morsels
      makes the mammy little too.

A little mouthful for the birdie.
A mouthful of little birdie.
Our faces fall
and the very thought of it
crumbles
like a piece of bread.

One of the creatures, with glossy black feathers,
a beak the orange of the tropics and a tail like an Oriental
    screen
foretells fairer weather. It carries something
that is still moving. With kindness and care,
tenderly feeding the robust infant
little by little. Opaque, dull fellow-creatures
transformed by this act into beauty itself. Beyond
the birth-nest, the family tree.

And who knows? Maybe
we're looking at a
foundling.
Our laughter resonates,
familiar, secure,
curled in the
foetal position of our privilege.
I remember how your pulse quickened
when they told you that yes, finally,
they would give you that little girl to adopt.
Sshh. Silence, not a word.
No-one need know.
Let me change the more peculiar
features of my physiognomy.
Burn all photographs of a life before.
Better still, just cut my face out of them;

I still want to remember the rest,
family occasions, loved ones.

Errant carnival, sunflowers,
appearances.
If people who love each other
end up looking alike,
then the same must be said for birds:
orphans of the same flesh and blood.

Passing through

The first
of the last
wings in the world.
PAUL CELAN

1

Birds of a cloistered dawn,
ever-present in love's captivity,
not knowing the open air
nor their own expansive movement.
Today they will be with you in Paradise,
savouring, sipping
wholesome juices
for the condor, the eagle,
the vulture.

2

The day the whole story
dawned on her,
she put an end with her own hands
to all her worst fears.
Abandoned her home,
elegant and perfumed,
while the church bells rang out
as they did every day,
then headed in the opposite direction.
She took a cage in each hand

and a psalm that rose up from them
heavenwards: *madre míaaaaa ...*
She came back as the sun set,
her hands dry,
sat on her rocking chair,
another cradle, another cage,
and never, ever woke again
to the commotion of departure.
Among humans,
this was known as falling silent;
among birds,
it meant a body can dispense
with palaces,
feelings,
signs.

Sacrifice

King

For I remember every thing:
there is no pleasure for me …!
NEZAHUALCÓYTL

Whose name signifies
all time,
a squandering of power.
Two wild beasts caged behind perfect muscles,
hungry lion, hungry coyote,
behind eyes that burn, insatiable, capable,
without even knowing,
of reaching beyond the domain
of rage.

Whose tears made a river
with those of his progenitor,
he, very small,
perched in a treetop,
to witness
the dread death of the guide of his dubitations,
who showed him the doors
to the reality
of a fair fight
with no adversary.

Whose kingdom was from that day on
like a dream of kindness, intense colour,

pleasurable at the heart
of a great desolation.

Whose awakening was at the hand
of someone, something, who led him
to the mountain of shifting mists
and covered him with the water of divine passion:
blood.
Baptized without submerging:
everything went inwards,
countless manifestations
of wars, cults, exquisite fruit,
few, very few words,
no hesitation.

Whose impetus addressed
the rose of the winds,
god of the near and the nigh.
And whose question persisted,
immersed in the visceral response:
is the faraway place that I sense,
the place of naked souls,
as beautiful as this?
The future pierces me
between the eyes.
It speaks of the place of bodiless ones,
that house of promiscuous divinity.
And the birds that came to drink
from this your well of discoveries,
from this deified heart of your poems,
from that instant
that you encountered with woman,
will find themselves bereft of the melancholy

they exchanged for freedom:
not even in death
will they leave you in peace.
They will go on devouring
imperatives,
your love for them:
"You will give pleasure (to the master of the universe)
this is the way to ask and seek (of the great Lord)".

Sacrifice

The goddess swallows herself,
and we in turn reveal
in equal parts
our misguidedness, our faith.

Approaching midday,
you described an evening,
an early morning
or a twilight;
so much time seemed
to have happened to you
in this place
that it could even be your life,
unrecorded,
or perhaps so little
that with every breath
you were still getting used to your surroundings.

For such realms to exist,
something that could be called a legacy,
a coded message,
the world must serve as our mirror.
And for the first flowering, the first fruit to be sacrificed,
we must be robbed of our daily bread.
Be apprenticed,
become an artisan
subsumed in the minutiae of the craft,
devoted to solving mysteries,
damp air,
delinquent atrocity.

Epimone

> ... *the overall effect, by which*
> *I mean the texture or soundtrack,*
> *not exactly the precision of great*
> *heights ...*
> EDUARDO MATA.*

If the last thing to go when we die
is our hearing,
then the maker of the canon
was brought back,
forged in red heat
as the voices came in,
each one repeating the
preceding songline.
Picking out from the eternity of a day
the scorpion's ritual course,
the shrill cry of its mate;
the cricket's delirium,
the competing minutiae
of all things
and the greatest, *ecce homo*:
the common end, death's nuptials,
intimacy of the gallows, crashing to earth,
having preferred the counterpoint
that pulses imperceptibly
in every inhaling and exhaling,
but never takes flight.

* *Eduardo Mata was one of Mexico's most distinguished orchestral*
conductors. He died in January 1995 when the plane he was flying crashed.

Sweetness

The sweetness of a classic
confection is never cloying.

Sounds, scattered
far and wide, vibrate,
suffusing
the skin's surface,
far-reaching pastures,
each with its own map,
its own zodiac.
Disarmed
by love and death,
present – here, there –
in lagoon or lake
where the sturgeon,
fine-toned, felicitous,
traces with its ascent
the silver threshold
of an ethereal *limen.*

Liquid
turquoise-hued emerald,
emerald-tinted turquoise.
This place, that epidermis.
A fitting corollary
of someone or something
who has navegated
their way through life
astride a stygian arrow.

Tense as a bow,
the string of love's subtle viola
releases feeling
and pulsates:

first,
by the dazzling beams of the lighthouses,
her anchors would sink
in a river of rivers, the Ouse,
with its Sanskrit roots,
that in the long run would weigh her down
more than the stones
in her coat pockets,
water
from which she would only emerge
through her mother and tongue,
the one true oracle,
an orality that springs and flows and oozes …
God be praised, in these bubbles we find
our primordial purpose, no doubt about it,
she discovered
in situ
the ever-virgin virginal virginia;

then
as luck would have it,
a redeeming return takes me
to my own *Lough Arrow,*
my latin-Southern-Central-American arrow,
Tequesquitengo,
trying to untangle myself from the
perfectly innocent seaweed, terrified,
swallowing more and more of the baptismal waters

of that Mexican Tiber.
Finally, the reeds
I would recognise fifty years later
as I plunged willingly, alone,
into other waves, caressed by other winds
that would devour and then deliver me up
in a deadman's float.
The name of that other lake, Arrow,
showed me its double edge,
the ancient spear and the legend:
Gae Bolga, peerless and terrible,
would shatter the moment
it entered the muscle
into a thousand splinters,
poisoned in the present,
still venomous in the future,
slowly sucking strength away.

In this and only this way
we once died of love,
bleeding on the inside.
Witnessed only by
those two watchful
and all-seeing words.

Schism

It happens.

Precisely in the body of a swan.
A big animal, the size of a healthy mammal,
a good-sized calf, nourished by the gaze
of everyday observers. None of the sharp corners of
    "earthed" creatures.
A swan has no hooves. Makes no enemies.
It died at the hands of a human. Beaten to death.
With a mallet, a useful kind of thing.
The mute, opaque blows of that tool turned weapon
on its flesh, its poor plumage as it slowly
turned red. Its blood. Its not responding,
its turning the other cheek with its whole body.
Its unquestioning innocence. Its why on earth would you
    wring its neck?
Its just because it's there final release, letting it fall;
beak first, like an anchor. The no reason why of its
    swansong, its candid
embrace of brute force beneath the setting sun.
It took more than twenty-four hours for it to depart.

Let me summon up spirits, the power of magic words:
take this great creature broken in pieces,
see it carried aloft in a pearl fisher's net.
Worthy of the white sheen of nacre.
Of transmigration.
Of what, now the spell is broken,
is swan inside.

Et in secula seculorum

Means embracing
beams of light
around the world
and the clay and blood
in the main atrium
of Arcadia,
where a body
finds pleasure foraging
amongst many-splendoured ideas,
crushing lesser creatures
in accordance with natural law,
feeling nothing,
then ingesting them
to neutralise the poison's effects,
and being subject to
the whims
of another intelligence,
slave to the self
that sits on a chair
on a rug
on a floor
on the earth.
For the love
of creatures.

The Snow-White Falls of Niagara

First Stage

Your picture postcard
crystalised
by a perceptible arc in the prism,
a tangible bow in the iridescent spray.
If it were a photograph
would you be watching from the fifth heaven?
From the balcony of your one
true
journey,
your powers of reflexion
poised in the nib of a pen:
the vocative case
got me
the fate I deserved,
Purita.

I made you feel the same way then
as I feel now, provoked by
the living creature that breathes before me,
a mortal soul.
I see him walking home from school,
carrying the burden of incomplete relationships,
whether cold or not it's all the same,
in a country both his and not his.
With the unspoken pressure
of a language that says a lot
and gives great pleasure,
adding to his baggage
the extra weight of frost -

baggage rightly claimed by a voice
rooted in a Slavic tangle unravelled from a delta
of Mozarabic, Ligurian and Spanish.
All praised be.

Second Stage

I trail my hand across a park bench
covered in snow
to freeze the memories
of you and me
in the town square
where all our loved-ones
talk
contentedly,
surrounded by the charms
of an evening in Yucatán,
listening to the song of the lark
whose legs, as it rises,
sink the legs of that bench
deep,
deeper into what we know as
birthplace.
And here, irony of ironies,
is where that other one ended up,
the one made of brick and flagstone.
Here it is
watching and waiting
with the patience of the dead
who outlive autumns,
leaves that no sooner adorn their branches
than they rot.

Third Stage

Leaning out over the railings
of my childhood palace
I pick you out
clear as daylight coming down the falls,
wishing you could paint them,
make me your eternal *hospes*,
abandoning yourself completely
to the greatest of Greek virtues.
And then, sitting side by side beneath
that torrent of water, my perfect dream,
or on the talismanic bench, I wonder
who is the visitor, who the stranger,
who is the foreigner,
the grass, nettles or greenness
of the marshes
that disappears, then tentatively
comes peering back out.
Or the frozen puddles where magpies
drill in search of treasure
on a perpetual one-way journey.

Or if it's all
mere illusion,
that one fine day
things will change.

Fourth and Final Stage

The face of old age
is hard to face,
that moment when everything

comes to nothing
and passion
inexorably goes under.
Better to wake up in any other scene
and say: what a morning.
Rainbow and all.
Park and all.
Farewells and all.
Signing off:
Sending all her love,
Your Mother.
The eighth wonder
thanks
to that third person,
(holy spirit)
of the singular.

Entre volcanes

Dramatis Personae

Mi voz se fue amoldando a sus tejidos.
Se detuvo. Creyó no poder más
y continuó.
Conoció así un cauce
nunca antes descrito,
unlugar del que era parte sin saberlo.
Al que volvió después.
Abrió sus puertas,
dio principio a los oídos.
Caracol de oleajes vigorosos,
saciaba todas las esperas
penetrando el cuerpo en rojo intenso.

Luego tu voz ventisca,
desde las copas
de bosques invernales,
de huertos de la tundra,
desde el encino, el cedro,
y desde el tamarindo,
atravesaba a los despiertos
que caminan
saboreando
la melodiosa sequedad
del trueno.

Stricto sensu

"No recuerdo gran cosa de mi vida privada"
INGMAR BERGMAN

En sentido estricto, nazco
bañada por el fulgor de una presencia.
Marcada entre el índice y el anular
de la mano derecha,
sobre la cima muscular que protege
la última falange.
Una montaña hizo a Mahoma dirigirse.
Y por más que me aferro a la Sierra Madre,
otra fuerza me imanta al descenso
de minutos y segundos
donde yo no era yo.
No era más que océano pulsando,
apaciguándose y siguiendo,
sin tocar el centro en llamas.
La idea de un hogar,
de hacer tumulto de los momentos más felices,
muñecas, cosas por doquier, objetos del engaño
ante dos imágenes poderosas: la purísima Concepción
y Santa Teresita con un ramo sin fragancias.
De hacer caso de la rabia.

Me dirigí a mi tristeza como a una habitación.
Y me encerré con llave. A piedra y lodo. Bajo cadenas
y candados. Y pronuncié *in*discernible.
*In*traducible hallé el torrente
de tinta *in*deleble.

Dolor de corazón

¿Por qué erráis solitarios
por las embarcaciones y el campamento
en medio de la noche inmortal?
ILIADA, X, 139

La laguna de los muertos no tiene fin.
También la llaman río, gran Estigio.
Fluye cautelosa, cauteloso,
encandilando a sabios y creyentes.
Es lecho de ilusiones, de rumores,
se aloja fácilmente enlos resquicios:
suelto espejismo
de humanos laberintos.

Intuyo su principio en esta barca, murmuré.
Sus tablones han dejado huellas en mis manos.
Los remos de la noche van hilando
la crisálida verdad del horizonte.

¿Es éste el ojo de agua
donde la diosa hundiera al hijo
para hacerlo innvulnerable,
brutal, indiferente?
¿Es éste el Verbo
de seco lagrimal
que arrojó escudos por la borda?

El fiel de la balanza

A Thomas Kinsella, el perfeccionista

Manos fantasmales envolvían
una suntuosidad
de selva en aquella isla pedregal,
el brillo sobre todo lo convexo.

Alguien había perdido la memoria:
el gran evocador de la tristeza,
única fuerza de los actos iniciales,
redactor de la epopeya.
Su ánima subsanó la herida obedeciendo,
dando la voz a cambio.

Esa tarde, me mostró una cicatriz.
Y dijo: sáciame con fuego.
Que rompa la madrugada
el iris,
resuelle
en pos
de su color.

Arúspice

He vuelto a soñarme en aquel tubo
de paredes lisas, obra magna,
en cuyo fondo me adentraba
en compañía de mí:
Vaya con Dios,
allá a lo lejos.
Ahora caigo en la vigilia,
en la cuenta de que nunca hemos salido,
tal como llegué a pensarlo;
que esos rostros que entonces,
¡oh, la infancia!,
creímos deformes reflejos
sobre el metal cóncavo de un muro,
eran sólo destilado porvenir.

Hubo una vez una soga
que alguien nos lanzó,
y alimentos que devoramos
sin saborear siquiera.

Hubo una vez el último mendrugo
acariciando el paladar enloquecido,
y sobre todo hubo palabras rebotando,
ellas sí tocando la lejana orilla de la luz.
Se asomaban y volvían,
gracia fiel, vaivén
tan intocable, nuestro.

Soñé también la eternidad.
Que las criaturas vivían siempre
dentro y fuera de sus meandros,
sin paredes tubulares,
promisorias letanías
retumbando entre los mientras y durantes.

Muy cerca de la superficie
de esta niebla, esta fortuna,
deseé.

Quise salvarme
en esos seres intocables.

Nomen est omen,
canturreaban para entonces.
Omen est nomen.

Prisma

Ansias de bienestar,
las vi recorrer el camino de costumbre,
el que va de la ciudad a alguna parte,
parte del mundo,
parte de mi adolorida humanidad,
grata aparición para quien me aguarda,
quien vive dentro de mí sin ser yo misma,
en mi sed, mis oscilantes momentos
de tribulación y paz.
Fui ellas. *Me* fui.

Suben a Chalma los peregrinos. Los que saben que la rama seca que van cargando echará flores a lo largo del trayecto. Son jóvenes en su mayoría. Llevan agua, un petate en que dormir y la cotidianidad de sus vidas a la vista. Hay viejos también. Niños sobre los hombros. El santuario avanza en busca de su sitio.

De golpe, con una pregunta
despertó su antigüedad.
¿Qué le piden al Señor
a quien veneran,
es decir,
a su cuerpo mortificado
por la fatiga de hoy
y la miseria de ayer?
Poder seguir llorando de rabia o de impotencia,
poder enfermarse más o excederse,
poder presenciar, vivir la aterradora falta de...

al centro del cuerno de la abundancia,
poder olvidar, sí,
al fantasma de los siete, ocho años
que arrebatado vuela sin cola o cuerda
que lo regrese a tierra,
olvidar la futura historia,
la nulas entregas amorosas.
¿Eso?
Oh, cuerpo, amo y Señor,
muéstrame un árbol creado a imagen tuya,
sinagogas, basílicas, mezquitas
cubiertas todas de ti siendo.

Se ha establecido el campamento. Es de noche. Grupos de
hombres por aquí, mixtos por allá, de mujeres con bebés
y niños más lejos. En torno a las fogatas, de pie, en
cuclillas. Comparte no el alimento ni el café, cada quien
trae su itacate, sino la razón de... y la celebran sentándose
en el suelo vil, dejando que las piedras se les entierren en
los muslos, dando de mamar al niño delante de quien sea.
El calor proviene de la cercanía de brazos, espaldas,
cuellos, senos: no del fuego: de la sangre. Hay quien cae
cormido, quien cabecea, quien vela. Ninguna necesidad
de techo.

Todos estamos destinados
al compás respiratorio
con que cantan las estrellas.
Comunión de astros es ésa,
recé con terror o envidia,
una cierta rotación,
una cierta traslación,
el gozo de lo indispensable.

Nada más.

Al día siguiente, llena de admiración y arrobo, regresé a esos lugares, deseando aspirar los últimos olores de lo que ahí se había soñado y compartido. Como quien vuelve a tocar la piedra votiva, los pies o las manos de la imagen gastada de algún santo milagroso:

No hallé sino basura.
La gran boca del Señor,
su mal aliento.

Sueño de música estelar

Para Beto y sus criaturas

Me dirigí a la ventana,
convocada por fuerzas irresistibles.
Mas no bastaba columbrar la escena desde ahí.
Había que ir al encuentro de una noche
de ópalo esparcido,
pintado con brocha gorda,
desaparecidas las fronteras,
cualquier atisbo de luz eléctrica,
cualquier silueta de casas, granjas,
humanas edificaciones.

Sólo murmuraban las estrellas:
se podía ver su movimiento,
escuchar su diálogo,
y éste
correspondía a fragmentos
que has cantado
y cantarás
hasta el final de los tiempos.

Un timbre personal
en exacta coincidencia
con el movimiento,
la posición, el cambio intergaláctico
de astros nacidos
para que la nota prolongada de una sombra,
a la que se pide consejo,

y la de una nota corta que responde de verdad,
seguida de un silencio necesario,
correspondan de manera natural
a un destello
sin ton ni son,
que hasta ofrezca una figura
a los ojos lejanos del intruso
que pide formas, sólo formas,
aunque fuera una silueta
de osas, canes, escorpiones,
seres reconocibles,
incapaces, pobres criaturas,
de abandonarse a la música del cielo,
ese abismal
devanar
de la madeja simple
de espacios
como éste.

Artículo de fe

En el poder del viento para dirigir la aurora
y su minúsculo destino
de un día en particular.
En las páginas y páginas que intentan
alguna definición.
Mientras ruge el *hacer* allá,
doblando árboles milenarios,
que besan el sagrado suelo que pisan.
Que los enciende y alimenta
e inventa su creciente y su menguante,
la copa frágil,
el follaje
burbujeante, desorbitado.
Femenina, una, masculino, el otro,
cercenados sus visos definitorios.

Todo tan cerca.
Avanzábamos inermes. Alcanzamos la cima
y nos volteamos a ver unos a otros.
Como Narciso, nuestra imagen
multiplicada en los estanques
del amor propio,
la sublime de antigüedad.
Creíbles.
Artículo de fe.

Entre volcanes

Haber nacido entre volcanes
aparentemente extintos.
Suelo que se agita por designio.

Un escalofrío. Un terremoto.
Alguien iba y venía
revisando si algún muro,
alguna lámpara
estarían por desprenderse
sobre los durmientes.
Podíamos perderlo todo.
Ni lo mande Dios.
Nos reduciremos a Pompeya.

Una desnuda circunstancia,
la de este tragaluz en invierno
me ha revelado el rumbo
tras la niebla.
La nieve se tornará deshielo
y la luz negación del miedo y la atrocidad.
Casa que traga la luz en un lengua antigua,
que es luz celeste en antigua lengua
y ventanal aquí.
La tierra prometida.
Verdadero tragaluz de noche.

Canción de cuna

Breve episodio

Acababas de retratar
a una niña despeinada,
de transida
aunque encubierta
mirada,
rodillas sucias,
El vestido le queda chico
y un nudo le ciega la garganta.
El cuerpo se transforma en algo
que uno no desea,
y termina en punto.

Canción de Cuna

al diapasón Ritter-Anguiano

Parábola el arrullo.
En tonos lisos empalma
con la lejanía del mundo,
la última grieta de la cueva,
este cráneo. Que resuena.

El eco
en tu cuerpo
todo oídos.
Tiempo de cuna.

1

Una niña, una niñita,
no apta para tonadillas tiernas,
tan de negra, de negrita.
Entre el primer año y el segundo,
tal vez ni eso. Que atención presta
al silbido que se asoma y se retira
del asombro de ese entonces.
Se siente *misma*,
por el frescor del viento tropical
que invade la "pieza"
inflando las cortinas, meciéndolas
a diestra y a siniestra,
crinolinas de ese quicio
y barcos que parten y abandonan

su estampa rumbo a un mar en las entrañas
cuyas olas no revienten
en el más allá. Que vuelvan
al alba.
Haya palabras,
luz y oscuridad con nombre,
certeza y lumbre:
vida mía.
Vida mía esto, vida mía lo otro,
vaivén de buque,
abanico que abre estelas
en la lozanía de su rostro.

No llores,
tu sal disolverá
estas espumas.

    Eres
    del aire, música
    que conservará dentro las arenas
    las que tus pies descalzos conocieron
    para no llevar a cuestas la congoja.
    Que las sombras te aligeren
    y coral y perla sean verdad
    ante el cambio total de la marea.
       La tempestad.

    2

Que si la vida se adelgaza,
sangre en aceite,
lienzo que se teje y se desteje

casi desde el primer
de acá para allá
de ti para mí
de la madre
a la tiniebla.
Del canto al muro.
El vientecillo sobre las sienes
aclara el paisaje.
Cuerda, estambre, hilo
y si la cabellera llega a ser así
un amasijo, una pelota
una maraña desértica en vuelo
rumbo a relatos llenos de pasión,
los inconclusos.
Rumor que enhebra lo de cada quien,
rumor que apresa no la arena,
el desierto mismo,
y vamos ya a la lluvia, al embrujo
entre sanar, enfermar, sanar y arrullo
milagro de recuperar la vista
entre un afligirse y otro.
Nada, nada, navega hasta amar.
Dormida
sal a tu encuentro. Sal de los mares,
las lágrimas, los espacios
mortales.

Y como ese ser de aire, de viento luego,
querrías sorber las mieles donde lo hacen las
    abejas,
no conformarte con menos, saberte huésped
de honor en el banquete de este huerto cerrado,
y como un loco que también se sabe tal
volar sobre el lomo de un murciélago,

no de un cisne, una paloma o un gorrión.
Sin acudir al cuervo.

3

Cuélgate aquí, en este regazo,
infante que anida
del nacer hasta el morir,
saliendo sólo a veces,
sólo furtivamente,
sólo por necesidad,
a sorber la tibieza del destino.

De aire, de mieles y de vuelos vivos
el regocijo en tu sonido natural.

Descansa, alteza
encerrada en una torre,
parpadea
ante escenas que valgan
la pena.
Cuerpo presente,
comienzan
a visitarte en tu ataúd,
a hacer ronda en torno a tu figura
sin poder tocarte
como a las cuerdas deslizantes
la vía láctea
de una lira, sarcófago
de quien se entierra vivo,
a quien se ha dado embocadura
para la emigración.

Piel tan fina, encaje de papel de arroz,
sin testimonios,
sin historia.

4

De la víspera de la gran batalla
hay huellas
en los cristales, en los muros,
en los pisos de claustros
donde tu versión de lo sublime
era el badajo de una enorme
campana de bronce.
Se te advirtió el recorrido:
por compañía tendrías
una canción de cuna
que pulsarías por dentro.
Nadie osaría interponerse:
por única vez,
manos a la obra.
Sin muertes en tu haber,
tributos incumplidos.

Abre las arcas, monarca.
Abre ventanas y sana.
Sé mundo mudo,
sin aldabones.

5

La nota final,
nota monárquica de invierno,

frío que se posa sobre sí.
Que acompaña a quien pregunta
y se pregunta cómo, con tal rabia,
elevará la belleza una plegaria
cuya acción no sea más fuerte
que una flor.
Llave de la torre.

Si me curara,
si sanara,
si pudiera mirar por el resquicio
sintiéndome entero aunque fugaz,
arriesgaría de nuevo la salud.
Que jugaría conmigo tarareando:
Hay amapolas
que pueden adornarte dentro,
entre tus campos y jardines,
delicias de ningún amo y señor.

Mejor verter líquidos mágicos
por los lagrimales
y:
solloce de alegría
la entraña infecta,
la guadaña.

Aire desencadenado,
manjar que se distancia
en cuanto la boca vuela.

6

Desde la caja de madera,
palo de rosa o palo escrito,
guitarra, cofre y urna,
germina un llamado al enemigo.
Estancia en espera del hechizo
que te hará libre
para henchirte de aromas embriagantes,
para armonizar sin yerro
y sentirlo.

Músico del curar,
sea tu acción la de la flor.
Fecunda la materia,
enciéndela, tienes la palabra:

Suscitare, hacer mover,
devolver el movimiento,
poner delante tuyo
un ánimo antiquísimo
con todos sus recuerdos.
Dios
de la muerte,
duerme inerme
entre informes brazos.
La cuna llama.

A duras penas

1

Hincada en un sillón de alto respaldo,
viendo llover.
¿Quién llueve?
Está lloviendo a mis seis años de edad,
acabo de escuchar por primera vez
con atención.
Acabo de aprender
a dividir esferas
y a quedarme inmóvil.
Paladeo, empañando el vidrio,
la distinta intensidad del aguacero, tormenta,
cortina líquida, tempestad,
chaparrón,
bolas enormes o livianas:
un sudar la gota gorda
un dar el cariño a cuentagotas.
Alguien sin expresión ondea como la bandera,
el que llueve, el que torna el acto inconjugable:
Lluevo yo, llueve Dios.
Al otro lado de esta cortina fresca,
mi madre conversa con su hermana.
La está consolando, para variar.
Porque ella es feliz, lo suficiente para ignorar
la lluvia,
para ser *de suyo* memoria involuntaria.
Su tic-tac.

2

La caída, el goteo sobre el patio de cemento
hace canastillas disueltas al instante.
Un poco más allá, sobre la superficie del estanque
disimula su imparidad. Se aúna.
Como hombre y mujer, una y la misma carne.
Delirio, paraíso, invisibles y visibles,
entre azul turquesa, blanco perla
y verde ala de mosca ondulando,
se me entierran en los ojos,
reverberación.
Como un balazo:

Por primera vez
un salón de clases, un plantel,
un cuaderno de iluminar.
De noche no concilio el sueño.
Demasiada agua sin lágrimas.
Demasiado a flote.
Me arrincono en la tibieza
de lo negro.
Pero veo todo. Lo creo.
Al darme vuelta, me topo con más agua,
tu ceguera.

3

De tus cuencas surge un río lodoso, constante, doliente
    caudal.
Andas dando vueltas como una desquiciada.
Intolerable la respiración acompasada de los demás,
que, dormidos, despiertan por dentro. Y perciben a

colores.

Prendes el radio. La estación te da la hora exacta cada
  minuto.

Habrías querido ensordecer.

Morirte y que valiera la pena.

En cambio, *a duras penas,* fluyen tus líquidos amargos
golpeándonos en pleno rostro,

excluyéndote a voluntad, vistiéndote de oscuro,

comiendo aparte, tiranizando con olores, hedores,
  aromas,

sin la peregrina idea de festejar alguna cosa.

Escrúpulo vivo.

Un todo en contra.

Un incesante duelo misterioso

como la virginidad de María, antes, durante y después
  del parto,

de dos filos esta daga, esta vulgar, común y corriente
  bagatela,

"este destino cruel que nos separa".

4

Descripción es revelación:
si vislumbras la verdad
y te revuelcas en ella
la harás desaparecer,
acaso hagas llover,
acaso seas quien llueve.
Hay que atarla al cuello
como soga de cadalso,
como escapulario.

Describir

Un músculo es el corazón,
un órgano que habla.
Expresa lo que ocurre afuera
invisiblemente por dentro.
Retrata a tamborazos,
en círculos concéntricos,
las distintas claves.

Revelar

Quito el velo, te doy a conocer,
te muestro en el paño de la Verónica.
Me figuro
en el pirul,
ese árbol inmenso, de tronco rugoso,
frutos que son flores, redondos, pequeños,
casi pura cáscara.
Dos niños entre sus ramas
se preguntan cosas, pelan y desgajan
la curiosidad, sacan jugo
a lo que sí y a lo que no entienden,
queda la sustancia entre los dedos,
pegajosa confidente.
De ahí mismo se amarraba una cuerda
que sostuvo piñatas incontables
o sirvió de liana.
Lancé un alarido, previéndolo todo,
y alcancé a elevar la vista al cielo:
las ramas del pirul, plenas.
Ambidiestros,
nuestros secretos.
De dos caras, escapularios.
Nunca volvimos a hablar de esa manera.

Algodón

Las olas, mar picado,
de los campos de algodón
en Georgia, en Alabama,
esa planta malvácea, según erudita
descripción de mi padre,
cuyo fruto es una cápsula
que contiene varias semillas
envueltas en una borra blanca.
Me hacían gracia estos detalles
de manual antiguo de botánica
con sus grabados *ad hoc*,
en combinación con la borra
manchada de aceite,
abandonada en un rincón de la cochera.
Las olas de este prodigio
entrelineadas en las confesiones de Nat Turner
y las orlas del vestido
de una joven madre
que me llevaba de la mano.
Ella subió al camión primero.
Por eso pude recorrer, en una travesía
interminable, microcosmos en eco,
sus zapatos de tacón alto,
sus medias con costura atrás
y el vestido de algodón.
Estampado, ligero,
apropiado para quien viene de provincia,
de tierra caliente.
Pregunté: ¿es nuevo?
Ella sonrió, pero yo regresé,
como de rayo, al corredor del segundo piso,

a sus pasos y a la cinta métrica de colores
colgándole del cuello. Al patrón de papel biblia
desplegado sobre la mesa de tareas.
No se diga más.

Escúchense, sí, y con sumo cuidado,
las notas que venían flotando, sólo para mí,
al mismo tiempo, desde la casa de la esquina
donde iniciamos aquel viaje. Volteé, y ni los vuelos
del algodón o su instantánea y evocadora procedencia
en geografías tan propias de su acento
me lograron distraer de aquella música y su letra:
"Presta oído a la elevación de nuestra voz".
Yo no sabía alemán y, sin embargo,
cinceladas en la mente tengo
Höre wie wir, die Stimme erheben,
er he-e-e-e-e-E-e-e-e-E,
etcéteras de un canto que no miente,
que no remite a Dios
ni a las plegarias que fui aprendiendo
de labios de esa misma mujer después,
sino a la deslumbrante
albura
de un vegetal,
el algodón,
la tela que de él provenía,
y el dibujo cacofónico de sus flores
estampado en la sensualidad urbana
de otras épocas.

Adoptivo

Al hablar de ciertos niños de mirada triste,
hábitos extraños, "mañas", olor a rancio,
no a jabón "Maja" o al posterior "Palmolive"
de la gran ciudad y la educación
como Dios manda,
se empleaba en la mesa
el término "adoptivo".
Yo estudiaba esa semántica.
Me quedaba patinando en tal gramática.
¿No se referirán a un pequeño
que ha sido adoptado? Demasiado fuerte el participio.
Nunca será lo mismo decir que alguien es
su hijo adoptivo que hablar de un tal por cual,
y concluir: es adoptado.
En un "ado" sin hache muda (con hache invidente)
quedaba quien había venido al mundo
porque nadie supo qué hacer para que no.
Los tutores serían castellanamente rígidos.
Huelga decirlo.

Qué distintas las historias de quienes vivían
la misma situación ignorándola hasta cierto punto
y hasta cierta edad, en que sobrevenía la revelación de los
    misterios.
Amor: enigma: llaves del reino
ex abundantia cordis. A éste le provocaba
un tumbo la noticia. En el mejor de los casos,
eran adoptivos. Y aquel buscar semejanzas entre mis cejas
    y las tuyas
o entre nuestras cabelleras, en un tris,
probaba un cabal "hacerse las ilusiones".

En torno a la mesa,
nosotros cuatro.
Físicamente, no dibuja
un círculo este mueble,
pero como si lo hiciera.
Cuánta luz.
Miramos nuestro parque.
El prisma
no requiere explicaciones.

Unos cuantos brotes nuevos de lilas silvestres,
algunos narcisos ya marchitos, incipientes tulipanes.
Tres árboles de la misma altura, o estatura,
gigantes adolescentes en competencia.
El de en medio, bien distinto, tiene sobre sí
la invasión de una enredadera que ha abierto nichos,
que a su vez cerrarse pueden, a las aves migratorias.
De pronto:

¿Ven ese pajarito gordo,
café opaco?
Trina
el diminutivo.
Es un bebé
en espera de su madre
que, día con día,
le consigue bocadillos.
También una expresión
que empequeñece
a la antigüita.
Pajarito bocadillo. Bocadillo de pajarito.
Lo imposible, cual migaja de pan,
se desmorona

literalmente
en nuestros rostros.

Uno de esos seres, de brillante plumaje negro, pico
color naranja tropical, cola cual biombo de Oriente,
en espera de propicias temperaturas. Lleva algo
que aún se está moviendo. Cuidadosa, bondadosa,
tiernamente lo va ofreciendo al robusto infante
poco a poco. Congéneres opacos y sin gracia alguna
se transforman en la hermosura misma. Más allá
del nido original, del árbol genealógico.

Quién sabe. Acaso
se trate de un hijo
adoptivo.
Retumban nuestras carcajadas
familiares, seguras,
acurrucadas
en el privilegio.
Recuerdo tu pulso acelerado
ante la noticia de que al fin
te darían aquella niña en adopción.
Shh. Silencio, ni una palabra.
Que jamás se entere nadie.
Cambiaré incluso ciertos rasgos
de mi tan peculiar fisonomía.
Quemaré todas las fotos anteriores.
Mejor aún, recortaré mi rostro
solamente, porque lo demás,
las fiestas, la familia,
sí lo quiero recordar.

Carnaval itinerante, tornasoles,
apariencias.
Si la gente que se ama se parece,
hablando de pájaros no cabría la menor duda:
una y la misma sangre en orfandad.

De paso

Las primeras
de las últimas
alas del mundo.
PAUL CELAN

1

Aves del claustro
de la primera luz,
las vivas siempre
en el cautiverio del amor,
las sin el aire libre,
las sin el amplio movimiento.
Hoy mismo estarán contigo en el Paraíso,
disfrutando, sorbiéndose
cual jugos nutritivos
para el cóndor, el águila,
el buitre.

2

El día que la mujer
se dio cuenta de todo
puso término por propia mano
a sus temores más profundos.
Abandonó la casa,
elegante y perfumada,
al escuchar las campanas
del templo cotidiano,
pero con rumbo bien distinto.

Una jaula en cada mano
y un salmo que desde ahí
ascendía: madre míaaaa...
Regresó al atardecer,
las manos secas;
se sentó en su mecedora,
otra cuna, otra jaula,
y no volvió a desperrtar
al estrépito del viaje.
Diríase, entre humanos,
que fue clavando el pico.
Entre pájaros,
que alguien decide prescindir
de alhambras,
emoción,
emblemas.

Sacrificio

Rey

¡Todo lo recuerdo:
no tengo placer...!
NEZAHUALCÓYOTL

Cuyo nombre significa
todo tiempo,
derroche de potencias.
Dos fieras encerradas tras músculos perfectos,
león y coyote hambriento,
tras los ojos rapaces, capaces,
sin saberlo,
de llegar allende el territorio
de la ira.

Cuyas lágrimas hicieron un río
con las de su progenitor,
él, muy pequeño,
encaramado en la copa de un árbol,
presenciando
la muerte atroz del guía de sus dubitaciones,
quien le mostraba las puertas
de la realidad
en buena lid
sin adversario.

Cuyo reino quedaba de ahí en adelante
como un sueño de bondad, color intenso,
disfrutable en el fondo
de una gran desolación.

Cuyo despertar fue de la mano
de alguien, algo, que lo conducía
hasta el monte de las sutiles nieblas
para cubrirlo con el agua del ardor divino:
sangre.
Bautizo sin sumergir:
todo iba dentro,
múltiples señales
entre guerras, cultos, frutos exquisitos,
pocas, poquísimas palabras,
nada de vacilaciones.

Cuyo ímpetu se dirigía
a la rosa de los vientos,
dios del cerca y del junto.
Y cuya pregunta quedaba
inmersa en la respuesta visceral:
¿será así de bello el lugar
que intuyo allá a lo lejos,
el de los descarnados?
El futuro se me clava
en el entrecejo.
Remite al lugar de los sin cuerpo,
la casa de la liviandad
de la divinidad.
Y las aves que llegaren a beber
de este tu pozo de los descubrimientos,
de este corazón endiosado de tus versos,
de ese instante
que conociste junto a la mujer,
descubrirán el robo de la melancolía
a cambio del desasimiento:
ni con la muerte
te dejarán en paz.

Seguirán devorando
imperativos,
tu amor por ellas:
"Daréis placer (al dueño del universo)
ésta es la forma de pedir y buscar (al gran señor)".

Sacrificio

La diosa *se* traga,
merced a ella mostramos,
en iguales proporciones,
nuestra errancia, nuestra fe.

Cerca del mediodía,
describías un atardecer,
una madrugada
o un crepúsculo;
te parecía haber pasado
tanto tiempo en este sitio
que podía él mismo ser tu vida
sin registro,
o quizá tan poco
que al respirar
te acabaras de adaptar al exterior.

Para que haya reinos tales,
algo que se llame herencia,
mensajes cifrados,
habrá de ser el mundo nuestro espejo.
Y para inmolar primicias, primeros frutos,
habrá que quitarse el pan de la boca.
Aprendiz volverse,
persona
inserta en los pormenores del oficio,
aplicada a resolver misterios,
la humedad del aire,
la delicuescente atrocidad.

Epímone

Si lo último que muere
es el oído,
el creador del canon
se rehizo,
se forjó al rojo vivo
con la entrada de las voces,
cada una repitiendo el canto
antecesor.
Distinguió, en el día eterno,
la caminata ritual del alacrán,
el chillido de su hembra,
la cigarra delirante,
la minúscula contienda
de todo lo que existe,
y la mayúscula, *ecce homo*:
fin compratido, muerte en connubio,
cadalso íntimo, estrépito,
por haber preferido el contrapunto
que late imperceptible
en cada inhalación y exhalación.
Pero no levanta el vuelo.

Dulzura

De un clásico manjar
que no empalaga

Rumor esparcido
cuan largo y amplísimo vibra,
confundiéndose
con cualquier otra epidermis,
extensos pastizales,
cada una con su mapa,
su zodíaco.
Anónimo,
esencial.
Inerme
ante amor y muerte.
Que son - ésta, aquél -
laguna o lago
donde el sollo,
el esturión melifluo,
logra en su ascenso
la raya de plata
de un *limen* etéreo.

Líquida
esmeralda aturquesada,
turquesa esmeraldina.
Este sitio, esa *cualquier otra epidermis*.
Secuela de algo o alguien,
propia del haber bogado,
navegado de por vida
en saeta estigia.

Como un disparo,
la cuerda de sutil viola de amor
desentume la emoción
y pulsa:

primero,
a la gran deslumbrada por los faros;
sus anclas se sumergirían
en un río de ríos, *Ouse,*
que pesaría a la larga
más que las piedras
en las bolsas de su abrigo
por parentesco sánscrito,
agua,
de la cual ella no emergería
más que por su madre y lengua,
único oráculo real,
oralidad que mana, rezuma, supura...
Dios Santo, en estos borbotones se halla
nuestro primordial sentido, no cabe duda,
descubrió
in situ
la siempre virgen virginal virginia;

luego,
por suerte,
me conduce en salvador retorno
a mi propio *Lough Arrow,*
mi flecha latino-sud-centro-americana,
Tequesquitengo,
tratando de zafarme de las algas,
ellas inocentes, yo horrorizada,
tragando más y más de las fuentes bautismales

de aquel Tiberiades morelense.
Por fin, los carrizales,
que cincuenta años después reconocería
al clavarme sola, por voluntad,
entre otras ondas, caricias de otros vientos
que me devorarían y devolverían entera,
flotando de muertito.

El apelativo de aquel otro lago, *Flecha*,
me mostró sus dos puntas, sus dos ojos
de lanza antigua, de leyenda:
Gae Bolga, única y terrible,
que al adentrarse entre los músculos
se subdividía en múltiples navajas
envenenadas en presente, ponzoñosas en su porvenir,
que sorbían los poderes lentamente.

Así, sólo así,
se moría de amor,
goteando dentro.
Sin más testigo
que esas dos atentas
palabras oculares.

Cisma

Hay tal.

Justo en el cuerpo del cisne.
Un animal enorme, del tamaño de un mamífero robusto,
de una ternera ya crecida, alimentada con miradas
cotidianas. Sin la dureza de lo que "hace tierra".
El cisne carece de pezuña. No mete cizaña.
Murió a manos de un ser humano. A golpes.
Con un mazo, algo útil.
Los choques sordos, opacos de este utensilio vuelto arma
sobre su carne, su pobre plumaje que, lentamente,
se va tiñendo de carmín. Su sangre. Su falta de respuesta,
su otra mejilla en todo el cuerpo.
Su clara condición. Su para qué torcerle el cuello.
Su porque sí del soltarlo, dejarlo caer;
el pico, un ancla. El porque no de su canto, su entrega
a la fuerza bruta bajo el sol poniente.
Tardó más de veinticuatro horas en partir.

Conjuro, palabras mágicas, vengan a mí:
llévense este animalazo hecho pedazos.
Entre varios hombres lo han cargado en una red
de buscador de perlas.
Digna de brillos blancos nacarados.
De transmigración.
De, roto el hechizo,
cisne por dentro.

Et in secula seculorum

Significa abarcar
los brillos del fanal
del mundo
y el lodo y la sangre
sobre el atrio principal
de Arcadia,
donde la persona
suele disfrutar paseos salvajes
entre el esplendor de las ideas,
aplastar seres menores
según los órdenes de la creación
sin sentir nada,
e ingerirlos luego
para neutralizar los efectos del veneno,
ser objeto
a total merced
de otra inteligencia,
ser presa propia
sentada en una silla
sobre un tapete
sobre un piso
sobre tierra.
Por amor
a las criaturas.

Níveas cataratas del Niágara

Primera escala

Tu tarjeta postal
cristalizada
por un tangible arco en el iris.
Si se trataba de una fotografía,
¿estarías observando desde el quinto cielo?
Desde el balcón de tu único
y verdadero
viaje,
tu poder de reflexión
en la punta de una pluma:
el vocativo
me haría ver mi suerte:
Purita.

Comenzaba a provocarte
lo que hoy exhala frente a mí
una criatura semejante,
un prójimo.
Lo veo venir caminando de la escuela
con la carga de sus relaciones incompletas,
frías o no, da igual, en un país suyo y ajeno.
Con el esfuerzo entre dientes
de una lengua que mucho significa
y placer causa,
añadiendo carretadas de escarcha al equipaje.
De quien merece reverencias
por proceder de una madeja eslava
que se desenreda en pos de un delta

mozárabe, ligur y castellano.
Alabanzas.

Segunda escala

Paso la mano por la banca del parque
cubierta de nieve
para congelar la remembranza,
a ti y a mí
en la plaza
donde todos los seres queridos
conversan
plácidamente
entre delicias
de una tarde yucateca,
escuchando los llamados de la alondra
cuyas patas, al alzarse,
hunden las de aquel asiento
hondo,
hondo en lo que se sabe
terruño.
Aquí cerca, ironías de la vida,
vino a quedar aquel otro, hecho de losa
y ladrillo. Helo ahí,
espera y aguarda, en calidad de muerto
que sobrevive
otoños,
hojas que más tardan en adornar
que en descomponerse.

Tercera escala

Embrocada en el barandal
de mi infantil palacio
te reconozco
en franco descenso por las cataratas
queriendo pintarlas,
haciéndome con ello
tu eterna *hospes*,
entregándote de lleno
a la mayor de las virtudes griegas.
Y luego, ya sentada junto a ti
bajo ese chorro de agua,
mi sueño dorado,
o en la banca talismán, me pregunto
quién es visitante, quién forastero,
quién extranjero,
la hierba, las ortigas o el verdor del páramo
que se esconde y se asoma, vuelve.
O los charcos congelados donde las urracas
taladran en busca del tesoro
de un perpetuo camino de ida.

Que es ilusión de que
un buen día
las cosas cambien.

Cuarta y última

Qué duro
el rostro de la vejez
que no tuviste,
ese instante

en que ya nada funciona bien
e inexorable
la pasión
abisma.
Mejor despertar en cualquier otro panorama
y decir: qué mañana.
Con todo y arco iris.
Con todo y parque.
Con todo y despedidas:

Te *quiere* mucho,
Tu mamá.
La octava maravilla,
merced
a la tercera persona
(espíritu santo)
del singular.

Sources

Sources

The original Spanish poems were first published in the following collections

Part I

Dramatis Personae	*Intemperie*
Stricto Sensu	*Tragaluz de noche*
Heartache/Dolor de corazón	*Intemperie*
Precision Balance/El fiel de la balanza	*Tragaluz de noche*
Soothsayer/Arúspice	*Intemperie*
Prism/Prisma	*Intemperie*
Dreaming of Star Music/	
Sueño de música estelar	*Santo y seña*
Article of Faith/Artículo de fe	*Tragaluz de noche*
Among Volcanoes/Entre volcanes	*Tragaluz de noche*

Part II

Brief Episode/Breve episodio	*Tragaluz de noche*
Cradle-Song/Canción de cuna	*Tragaluz de noche*
Painstaking/A duras penas	*Tragaluz de noche*
Cotton/Algodón	*Tragaluz de noche*
Foundling/Adoptivo	*Tragaluz de noche*
Passing Through/De paso	*Intemperie*

Part III

King/Rey	*Tragaluz de noche*
Sacrifice/Sacrificio	*Tragaluz de noche*
Epimone/Epímone	*Intemperie*
Sweetness/Dulzura	*Santo y seña*
Schism/Cisma	*Tragaluz de noche*
Et in secula seculorum	*Eter es*
The Snow-White Falls of Niagara/	
Níveas cataratas de Niágara	*Tragaluz de noche*